Cryptocurrency 2021-2022

Trading Tips & Investment Strategies for Beginners

STELLAR MOON PUBLISHING

Disclaimer

Introduction

The latest Bitcoin Crash

It can't have escaped anyone's attention: Bitcoin has taken heavy blows. Like any financial market, Bitcoin trading is led by emotion.

Or rather, the crypto currency investors are led by emotion and Elon Musk's recent tweets are causing a lot of FUD ("Fear, Uncertainty, Doubt"). Completely unexpected, he attacked Bitcoin on fossil fueled energy consumption and carbon footprint.

Despite the fact that this story has been debunked many times, people are very sensitive to this, and when such a big celebrity shouts something, most people believe it immediately and fear gathers around. What does this mean for the Bitcoin price and other crypto currencies?

Stellar Moon Publishing compiled this book to offer an insight into the best trading tips and strategies for 2021. This book has been written by a group of cryptocurrency experts. With this book, we strive to provide you with the best curated information on cryptocurrency trading and investments.

Just as Bitcoin's price was recently rebounding the fear set in and the deflation was significant. The advantage is that the real solid support levels now stand out. In spite of all the panic: the $30,000 barrier appears not to be broken anytime soon. Not even Elon can break it down that far!

Meanwhile, most of the alternative cryptocurrencies see a bull run right now.

Since they're more attractive in terms of energy consumption, they might be that alternative to Bitcoin for trading value in the long term.

These coins that might have a stable future perspective are Cardano **(ADA)**, Stellar Lumens **(XLR)**, Ripple **(XRP)**, Solana **(SOL)**, EOS **(EOS)**, and Tron **(TRX)**.

In this book we'll talk more about how these individual coins work, why Bitcoin will stay strong in the long term future and why these alternative coins could become a substantial part of the crypto market.

The Cardano price doesn't wait for investors to buy into the dip

To start of with a bit of a preview, on May 5th, 2021, Cardano broke out of a rising pattern that had formed over the past months. The breakout occurred with a remarkable jump in market volume. This marked a trend change for the altcoin. That coin had shown little price action for the past two months. Despite the huge crypto crash caused by Elon Musk, ADA is holding up great. In fact, the price is up by 6% recently.

An even bigger crash in the crypto market is the only thing that could prevent a push to the $2.27 mark.

Around $1.57 lies significant support for Cardano in the future. More people will buy in once they see that a higher price point seem to stabilize. Therefore, there is no chance that the price will fall much further than this level.

Pump and dump schemes are as popular as ever

With coins such as Dogecoin, Shiba coin and Safemoon dominating the crypto marketing in terms of investment profits, a lesson should be taken that following and buying into trends purely based on the amount of money that could be made in a short term is as risky as ever.

Table of Contents

Our books

Check out our other book to learn more about NFTs, NFT trading and selling, how to make profit and essential tips and strategies for a fail-proof start in the NFT universe.

Join the exclusive Stellar Moon Publishing Circle!

You'll get instant access to the mailing list with updates from our experts every week!

Sign up here today:

https://campsite.bio/stellarmoonpublishing

Pump and dump schemes

It's never a good idea to mindlessly follow a hype of a random coin, just because people claim to have made huge profits over night.

This generally indicates towards a "classic" pump and dump scheme, meaning that in order to make massive profit with a crypto coin, use the influence of news, crypto blogs, youtubers and other influencers, social media platforms such as Reddit and Facebook to hype up the price of a seemingly random coin.

The general idea of this is to buy in early and dump the amount of coins bought as the price rises a 1000-fold.

It's easy to recognize this pattern as the claims are usually in a trend as follows:

Random shitcoin launch price is $ 0.000001 with the claim that if this coin will climb to $ 0.001, you would make around 1000x profit.

These claims about random coins that are about to burst are all over the internet; Tiktok, Instagram, Facebook and Reddit are swarming with paid and unpaid advertisements regarding pump and dump schemes.

All of this simply means, whoever is in on it, can get massive profits as long as they get enough people to buy into the hype.

Influencers get paid to push this information.

It can pay up to $ 25,000 per post if you're an influencer willing to promote one of these schemes. Because if you build up a decent number of followers, there is a greater possibility that people will buy into whatever you have to tell them.

And as a content consumer, and someone who is looking to buy into the next hype, critical thinking is your best asset.

Dogecoin

The prime example of a pump and dump with social media influence, is what Elon Musk did with Dogecoin and Bitcoin, a couple of tweets and mentions about both coins, and as you probably saw in recent news, the price of Bitcoin and Dogecoin rises, and he bought in, especially into Bitcoin, before he started the rumor, he probably made a billion in profits from simply mentioning it in a tweet, same as he recently caused a crash in the Bitcoin price.

Elon Musk is a smart man in that regard, follow his investment strategy, where he buys up a massive amount of Bitcoin, claiming that his company Tesla, will now accept Bitcoin payments for the cars and drives up the price by a massive margin, an all-time high of over $60,000.

And not much later, Elon Musk drops a bomb, telling the internet that Bitcoin mining is terrible for the environment, meaning he sold out at the high price point, watched the market crash, and creating a new entry point for people to buy in.

He started to tweet about Dogecoin in early April, with the starting price around $0.05, and on 16th April, the price hit an all-time high of $0.39.

A short dip followed, the coin dropped back to $0.19 on April 23rd and after that it continued to rise back up towards a new high of $0.71 on May 5th, followed by another drop with the current price at $0.50.

There is not too much to say about the future of Dogecoin as it feels like some kind of joke. Elon Musk has proven himself in the past to be a big fan of internet culture, and have a currency such as Dogecoin, rule the financial market is nothing more than an elaborate joke.

So, if you feel lucky, you could buy in on Dogecoin and take the gamble that will double in price in the near future, but any success is entirely based on luck with a coin that has its price based on speculation. So, in essence investing in certain cryptocurrency is a bit of a gamble.

A good rule thumb if you're willing to gamble with pump and dump schemes is to buy in when the rumors start and start selling when it hits the mainstream news.

Since the price will quickly rise whenever a trending coin hits the mainstream news channels, it also means that a lot of people that bought in early, use this moment to cash out, sell the coin and get the profit, causing an almost immediate price drop when a large number of coins get sold on any of the markets.

Meaning that if you don't have solid information on when this dump will happen, you're bound to lose your stake, if you're late. Since cryptocurrencies are decentralized, they're basically impossible to regulate as long as the information gets out and trending.

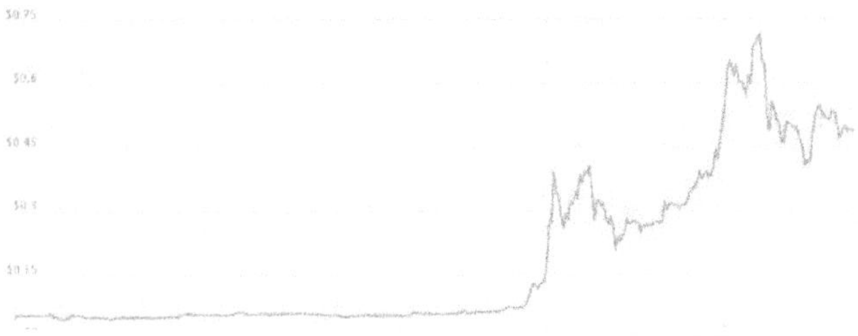

Intrinsic value of cryptocurrency

Don't buy into new or relatively unknown coins as a long-term investment if they don't show any intrinsic value.

So, a solid piece of advice would be to know what you buy into, do you know if it is a so-called "shitcoin", a marketing scam that people use to drive up the price, or if the coin has real application value.

For example, Ripple (XRP) aims to become the next global payments network for financial institutions. If you follow the news around Ripple, it is a bit easier to predict what the price will do, right now they have a 40% stake in Asia's cross-border payments system and they work hard to solidify their future as a financial instrument.

Right now, creating a new coin takes about 5 minutes if you want to create a pump a dump scheme. Next up will be marketing, make sure people get know that your coin will be the next one that makes them rich and gain interest on the internet.

This coin has to be coin that doesn't need proof of work like Bitcoin does as explained in the chapter "**The Intrinsic Value of Bitcoin**".

So, if you want to start a coin yourself, make a copy of an existing coin that requires no effort to trade and start up, you could probably find a tutorial for setting this up on YouTube.

Call the new coin anything that with keywords such as safe, or going to the moon, such as the infamous Safemoon, claim that it's going to burst, and make sure as many people as possible need to hold on to that coin because it will make them rich. Preferably implementing a hefty fee if they want to sell it.

Publish a white paper about your coin; a white paper is an explanation of how the coin works, how to buy it and other vital information to get the interest of investors.

For a pump and dump scheme, this would ideally be a paper that claims some kind of transaction fee that gets paid out to the coin holders. The idea behind this transaction fee that pays out to the other coin holders is to create a sense safety for the potential investors.

If a new person buys some coins and they get their friends to buy some coins, everyone seems to profit from such a system. They want to create an illusion that if you get as many people as possible to buy that coin, everyone gets rich.

However, one crucial part that would make that possible is that the coin needs intrinsic value. If you need to buy in and keep the coin in order to gain value, it will be discouraging to sell them for dollars as in essence the price would drop.

15

And simply put, it's a dead system if the value has to come from people that have to buy in. That system only indicates, that once, enough people have bought in, the owners and large coin holders can sell out, make the value of that coin drop while other the people that are not in on the moment of selling out take a loss.

To put it into an example;

If person A buys 10 coins and you have a 10% transaction fee, 1 coin of these coins get divided over the other coin holders, so if there are 10 coin holders at this point, all of them would get 0.1 coin from that transaction.

Many of the scam coins that get promoted right now, they boast a similar type of system as explained the example, promising they will explode in value if enough people buy and everyone gets a share when someone buys in.

If you paid attention and read between the lines, you would have made the conclusion that this is the cryptocurrency equivalent of a pyramid scheme.

Safemoon and Shiba Inu: scam projects?

For those of us who have been following the crypto market for a while, we know that the bull run of 2017 and 2018 was accompanied by a slew of coins that were not only as volatile as Bitcoin, but also as volatile as the day Bitcoin crashed.

These scam projects, or shitcoins as some call them, give crypto a bad reputation, but it appears to be a good part of the industry as new technology. With all of the hype surrounding Bitcoin and Ether, we must keep in mind that a variety of smaller coins will also rise in value.

 As we explained previously, pump and dump schemes such as the infamous Safemoon, are basically the cryptocurrency equivalent of a pyramid scheme.

With the rapid rise of the Shiba coin, many people are wondering if a crash is imminent. As Binance announced earlier recently, the top #1, #2 and #5 wallets contain 50.5%, 7.0% and 3.0% of the total supply respectively, which would normally be extremely worrying, but in this case it's an even stranger story.

The developers at Shiba Inu sent 50% of their tokens to Ether founder Vitalik Buterin at launch.

We are a bit positive about the Shiba coin at the moment but it seems that because of the false sense of security, a situation is created with a low threshold to risk your money.

We predict that this coin will also be very volatile and will probably see a future as one of thousands of pump and dump projects.

Binance has also listed SHIB in their Inovation Zone, making it possible to buy Shiba Inu through the exchange (which can only be done after filling out a questionnaire).

However, Safemoon currently has over 1.9 million users, but Binance refuses to listen to it. While the CEO Changpeng Zhao previously said that when a project has a large number of users, they will listen it. There are more Safemoon users than at Shiba, also Safemoon provided a record number of transactions on the Binance Smart Chain.

The intrinsic value of bitcoin

Bitcoin has intrinsic value in its transaction. A Bitcoin transaction is a calculation, and doing that calculation gets a reward, a block, a Bitcoin, hence why it's called the blockchain. Since each Bitcoin transaction is a calculation that consists of every other calculation (consisting of previous transactions) leading up to the transaction.

So, since Bitcoin has been in use since 2009, these countless transactions have led to the point where it takes an immense amount of calculation power to complete a transaction. Doing these calculations is called mining, and it's a business where Bitcoin mining requires more electricity that a small country at this point.

In order to have the Bitcoin crash completely, people would have to stop trading it at a point in time where one transaction would cost too much to calculate it. Hence this principle ensures the long-term future of Bitcoin as long as people use it to trade.

Also, Bitcoin has been the fundamental currency of the black market because the owners of Bitcoin cannot be tracked through personal account details like having a bank account, thus Bitcoin can be used to buy anything outside of the law.

There is no bank or financial institution holding account details and personal information about Bitcoin owners. And if you want to keep your privacy with the amount of

Bitcoin you own, it is advised to keep it in a physical wallet such as the Trezor One.

So, in order to keep your transactions as off-grid as possible, make sure to use an anonymous route of buying your Bitcoin, and keep them off trading platforms that require personal details in order to use them.

Bitcoin trading privacy

Trading platforms for Bitcoin might require access to personal details in order to use that platform, especially since the certain governments want to track these transactions.

The platform Binance is under investigation right now for tax fraud and money laundering by the U.S. government, purely because the U.S. government want to track who is trading and who owns what on these platforms.

They even offered platforms to pay for personal details, and even though many crypto trading platforms claim to have perfect customer privacy, it wouldn't be the first time, they sold personal data to third parties. There are even some rumors that certain platforms sell out to the government, but nothing can be said for sure.

Bitcoin was built to decentralize value. As far as the past can teach us, money rules the world, and if you control large sums of money, you have nearly infinite power.

Another rule is also true, that money indefinitely corrupts, money has been the cause of greed, egoism and poverty all around the world and it's in the hands of a very small percentage of people.

Bitcoin can be used to destabilize the global store of value if enough people buy into it. Classic banking is built on inflation in the current economic system and if enough money flows into the crypto currency market, it will destabilize the inflation of regular money.

Banks use the money that people store to invest in whatever they deem to be profitable; they also used a good part of that value to create loans such as mortgages.
But at this point they have to keep printing out money to keep the system running, because more loans means less actual value of money. And if you put the value next to the current global flow of money, it's a giant bubble of credit bound to burst.

Why bitcoin is a solid long-term investment

This bubble of credit portrays why Bitcoin is such a solid investment for the long-term future. With the total trading value of Bitcoin in dollars right now, the entire market of Bitcoin is valued at a staggering $846,019,261,238.40, or shortly said, 846 billion dollars.

So, Bitcoin has reached a value of almost 1 trillion dollars, and it's coming close to overtake the dollar, which has around 1.2 trillion dollars worldwide.

To put the crypto market in perspective, the total market capitalization is valued at 2.2 trillion dollars.

Consider that Bitcoin mining will become exponentially more difficult, requiring more processing power and more electricity over time as long as Bitcoin is used. Another important fact for the value of Bitcoin is that the amount of Bitcoin is finite, meaning that at some point in time the last Bitcoin will be mined, and it's estimated right now that it will take more than a 100 years.

This means that the price of Bitcoin is nowhere near the price that it will be in 20 or more years and with the current rate of inflation, it's an extremely desirable store of value for the long term.

It's a fact that the dollar will inflate more, it seems that it has to come to a crash at some point since at some point it will simply make the prices unreasonably high, rendering the dollar more worthless of the course of time.

You can see proof of this in the prices of crude materials such as wood right now. These prices are sky-high, and they are slowly starting to destabilize the housing market.
The cause of this is in the fact that Donald Trump put a massive increase on import tariffs on wood from China in 2020, creating a situation where the U.S. buys up all the wood from Europe, driving up the price immensely.

This makes that renovation, new housing and other projects that require large amounts of wood are becoming much more expensive, even so that it influences prices on the real estate market right now.

Houses have been more expensive than ever in Europe to the point where it starting to cause problems in other markets.

This means banks have to give out a much large mortgage for a smaller house than 10 years which will only contribute to enlarging the credit bubble and its effect in every aspect of the economy.

The current chip shortage

The biggest contributor to the store of value in Bitcoin is the chip shortage, Bitcoin is one of the driving factors of chips becoming more valuable and because of the higher demand it leads to an inflated price and shortage.

One of the speculations is that Elon Musk caused the crash because the chip shortage is also affecting the production of Tesla cars. So, disrupting the market price of Bitcoin, disrupts the market for Bitcoin mining equipment, this could potentially create a bit of space in the chip market.

A much-needed space for other manufacturers that really in one way or the other on chips and semi-conductors.

But the certainty remains that Bitcoin mining difficulty will increase as long as Bitcoin trading exists, demanding more from the chip market, and boosting prices for the equipment needed for Bitcoin mining.

Quantum computing will not have impact on Bitcoin mining

Simply put recent studies, done by Louis Tessler and Tim Byrnes, have shown that quantum computing cannot do Bitcoin mining more efficiently than current ways of Bitcoin mining. Hence, the proof of work from Bitcoin mining has a very stable future in the current computing environment without any threats that would make the proof of work in Bitcoin mining obsolete.

So, in conclusion, and taking in account all these different factors, it can be a very smart move for growing a long-term capital to invest a monthly amount of money in Bitcoin, that you would normally save on regular bank.

Cryptocurrency investment strategies

A good strategy to apply for holding Bitcoin or other cryptocurrencies is to only invest money that you do not need on the short term. Bitcoin for example, in its current state is still extremely volatile, and if you follow its course closely, and expecting only growth, you might be in for an emotional rollercoaster.

These are 5 steps for a successful Crypto Investment Strategy

Step 1: Decide how much money you want to invest

The first step to a successful cryptocurrency investment is always to determine the investment amount. Only when you know how much you want to invest in cryptocurrency, you can start developing an appropriate strategy for this. For example, if you only want to invest a small amount, then it may pay to choose the somewhat cheaper altcoins that you have done enough research on. It is crucial to understand what value the coin has within the financial system.

If you have more budget, then investing in Bitcoins, for example, could be an option. Therefore, always determine the investment amount in advance and make sure you don't deviate from it later on. It can be very tempting to invest more and more savings in cryptocurrency.

Although in some cases this can be smart (for example when you don't need the savings and you see nice investment opportunities), it is still important to keep sufficient savings in normal currency. This way, in case of an emergency, you don't have to immediately start selling cryptocurrency to be able to finance necessary (unexpected) expenses.

Step 2: Determine your appropriate investment strategy

Within investing in cryptocurrency, there are many different strategies imaginable. For example, you can choose to invest in the long term or in the short term. Which strategy suits you best depends entirely on your personal situation. Possible factors that may influence the strategy choice are, for example, how long you want to invest the money, how much time you want to invest yourself (daily or weekly) in your cryptocurrency and how much knowledge you already have about crypto coins.

There are generally two strategies you can follow when investing in cryptocurrency. The first strategy is to hold coins for a longer period of time in order to maximize profits. The second strategy is so-called day trading, where you buy crypto coins with the aim of selling them again in the short term.

There are generally two strategies you can follow when investing in cryptocurrency. The first strategy is to hold coins for a longer period of time in order to maximize profits. (long-term investment) The second strategy is so-called day trading, where you buy crypto coins with the aim of selling them again in the short term.

Set your goals

Trading stocks or cryptocurrencies is a big game between "Bulls" (buyers) and "Bears" (sellers). One group is betting that the price will go down while at the same time the other group is betting that the price will go up. Within Crypto Trading, you can roughly set two goals:

1. **Collecting more Bitcoin:** By trading Altcoins against Bitcoins, you ensure that you get more and more Bitcoin in your possession. People who choose this option trust that Bitcoin is going to become much more valuable in the long run, so they want to set as much Bitcoin as possible.
2. **Collecting more Fiat currencies (such as Euros, Dollars and more):** By trading Bitcoin or Altcoins against Euros, for example, you can ensure that you own more and more Fiat. This group of people use Bitcoin like any other tradable unit. So, they do not believe in the underlying value, but mainly find the volatility of the coin interesting.

Long term or Short Term?

The basics of trading and investing are easy: Buy cryptocurrencies when your price is low and sell them when the price is high. This is also called "long" in trading terms.
You can also do it exactly the other way around, sell your cryptocurrencies when the prices are high and buy back when the price has dropped. This is also called "Short" in trading terms.

Anyone who starts trading will basically always take a "long" position. You buy Crypto and sell it when the price is higher. Short positions are mainly used by experienced traders who also use leverage. However, we would advise against this for beginners, as it can also lead to you losing your money very quickly.

Step 3: Find the coins you want to invest in

Choosing interesting cryptocurrency, especially in the beginning, is probably one of the most difficult steps. When is it interesting to invest in a currency? When should I definitely not invest in a currency? If you knew the answers to these questions, you would be a millionaire within hours. Unfortunately, no one knows the answer to these questions 100% for sure, so in a way it always remains a gamble. but thanks to this book you have gained more insight into why Bitcoin can be a safe investment in the long run and how you can lose your money quickly by getting into a pump and dump scheme without prior knowledge.

So, by gaining enough knowledge about the coins you want to invest in, you can indeed make a good prediction. Of course, it's always smart to spread opportunities. Therefore, never invest in just one type of cryptocurrency, but spread your deposit at least over 2 to 3 different coins. Of course, it is also true that gaining knowledge remains an ongoing process. It is therefore not possible to say at a certain point that you have 'sufficient knowledge' of your coins and then not do any further research.

Step 4: The right moment

If you have been reading up on specific coins for a while, you probably already have an idea of the ideal purchase moment for yourself. To determine the ideal purchase moment, it is in any case wise to carefully analyze the prices of recent times. Often there is a clear pattern to be seen in the price developments of specific currencies. In addition, it is also important to determine the moment of sale.

When do you finally sell the coins again? The moment of sale is different for everyone. It depends entirely on the sales value with which you would be satisfied. Although the moment of sale is different for everyone, it is definitely wise to determine in advance at what price value you plan to sell your cryptocurrency. Of course, no one will ultimately force you to actually sell it for that value, but it does give you something to hold on to in the uncertain world of cryptocurrency.

Step 5: Ask for Help

Especially when you are just starting to invest in cryptocurrency, there are many things you won't know exactly yet. Although there is an enormous amount of knowledge to be found on the Internet, it can also definitely pay off to ask for help from the experts every now and then.

More and more financial advisors can provide excellent advice on investing in cryptocurrency. Of course, it is important to be critical when choosing a financial advisor. Costs are often high, but the right financial advisors who specialize in cryptocurrency cost nothing in practice. They provide far more profit than the cost of the advice you are spending.

At Stellar Moon Publishing, we work with a number of advisors who can provide you with appropriate advice to develop a profitable strategy for your crypto investments. Check out the contact options at the back of the book and let us know if you need help with your approach.

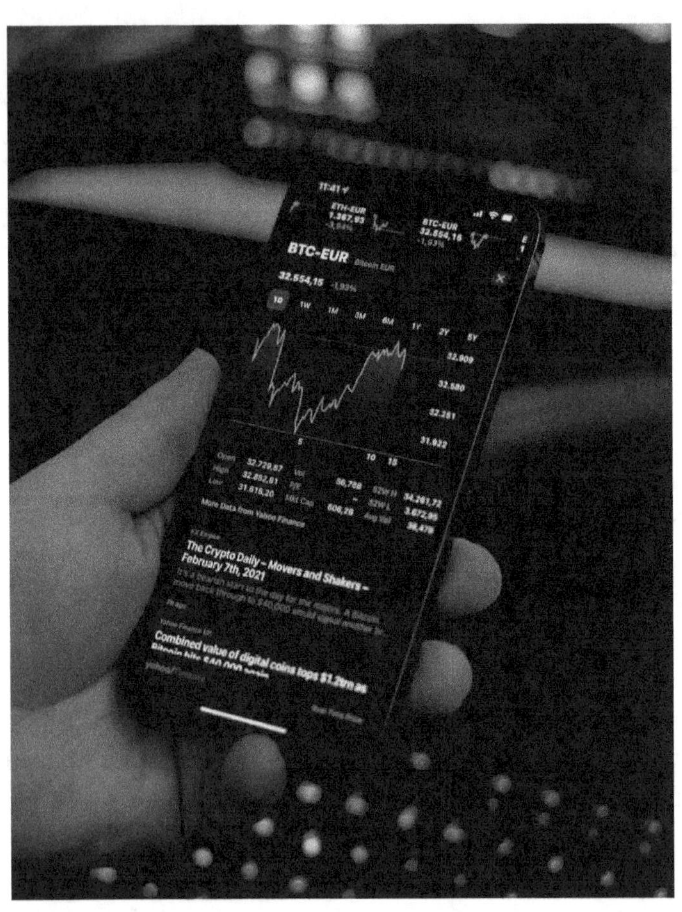

BTC-EUR
Bitcoin EUR
32.554,15
The Crypto Daily – Movers and Shakers – February 7th, 2021
Combined value of digital coins tops $1.20tn as

Essential tips for cryptocurrency success

The rules of safety are written in blood. This is a statement that every soldier who serves his or her country is familiar with. Although we are not discussing the risk to human life here, it is extremely inconvenient to lose your valuable Bitcoins due to mistakes made while you're trading and investing into crypto currencies.

Give each transaction a reason.

Only enter a **trading position**; *a price at which you want to sell or buy your coin.*

If you know why you want to sell or buy it and therefore have a clear strategy in mind.

Not all Crypto Traders can make a profit because this is a zero-sum game (where you make a profit, someone else on the other side loses).

Large coin holders (also called Whales in the crypto world) drive the alt & Bitcoin market - yes, the same "whales" responsible for buying and selling hundreds of Bitcoins at a time.

The whales patiently wait for unsuspecting small investors like us to make a trading mistake.

Even if you want to trade every day, it is sometimes better to do nothing than to jump into the rushing water and risk significant losses. Some days, you can make the most money by doing nothing at all!

Set clear goals and know when you need to stop

For each **trading position** you want to take, you must define a precise profit target level and, more importantly, a stop-loss level to limit losses.

Setting a stop-loss goal entails determining the maximum loss that can be accepted before closing the **trading position**.

Several factors must be considered when deciding on a stop loss level. The majority of traders fail because they "fall in love" with their position, meaning that the coins they hold, seem to go up in price, or they expect that it won't crash any lower, and they don't want to sell and take the profit/loss, or they fall in love with the cryptocurrency itself.

Meaning that no matter what, you choose to hold that coin for dear life. "I'm sure it will change, it will go higher, and I will exit this position with a minimal loss," they tell themselves. They allowed their ego to rule them.

In comparison to the traditional stock market, where 2-3% volatility is considered extreme, crypto transactions are much riskier: it is not uncommon for a cryptocoin to lose 80 percent of its value in a matter of hours. And you certainly don't want to be the one who is clinging to it!

Be aware of FOMO

Meet FOMO, which stands for "Fear of Missing Out." It's not fun to be on the outside looking in when a specific coin is pumped up like crazy with huge gains in just a few minutes.

That long green bar begs you to buy it, saying, 'You are the only one who isn't benefiting from this, so buy me!' At this point, you will also notice that many people and groups on Reddit, Telegram, and other platforms can only talk about this pump.

So, what are we to do? It's as simple as that: stay sober. True, the price may continue to rise, but keep in mind that the whales (mentioned above) are simply looking for small traders to sell their cryptocoins to.

Which they purchased at a lower cost. The price has risen, and it is clear that the coin is now in the hands of only a few smaller traders. Needless to say, when the coin is dumped in large quantities, the next step is usually a bright red price drop.

Risk Assessment

"Pigs grow fat; hogs are slaughtered." This quote tells the story of profit from the standpoint of success. To become a profitable Crypto trader, you should never seek out extremes. You seek out small profits that will add up to a large one.

Risk should be managed wisely throughout your portfolio. For example, you should never invest more than a small portion of your portfolio in a non-liquid (highly volatile) market. We will give those positions more leeway, and the stop and target levels will be set far away from the buy level.

Cryptocurrencies get traded for Bitcoin

This underlying asset causes market volatility: most altcoins are traded against Bitcoin rather than fiat currency (such as euros or dollars). Also see: What Is the Difference Between Cryptocurrency and Fiat Money?

Bitcoin is extremely volatile in comparison to almost any fiat currency, and this fact should be considered, especially when the price of Bitcoin fluctuates dramatically.

It was common in the early years for Bitcoin and altcoins to have an inverse correlation, which meant that when Bitcoin rose, altcoin prices fell relative to Bitcoin and vice versa. However, the correlation has become less clear since 2018. In any case, when Bitcoin is volatile, trading conditions become hard to determine.

Because we can't see far ahead during a volatile period, it's best to set close targets and stop-loss goals - or don't trade at all.

Use your alt-coins for trading

The majority of altcoins lose value over time. They can lose value gradually or rapidly.

However, the fact that the list of the top 20 altcoins has shifted so dramatically in recent years says a lot. Consider this when adding large amounts of altcoins to your portfolio for the medium and long term, and of course, choose them wisely.

If you are thinking about holding altcoins for the long term or building a crypto portfolio for the long term, pay close attention to the daily trading volume and conduct thorough fundamental analysis.

Altcoins with a thriving community have a good chance of surviving in the long run.

ICO, IEO, and token sales

Moving on to public ICOs (or IEOs, as they are now known in 2021): these are sales of crypto tokens. Many new projects choose to hold a crowd-sale, in which they provide investors with an early opportunity to purchase some of the project's tokens at a lower price.

The incentive for investors is that when the token hits the market, they will be able to profit handsomely. Many successful token sales have occurred in recent years, with ROIs of 10x not uncommon.

The Augur ICO, for example, provided investors with a 15x return. So, what's the catch? Not all of these projects return a profit to their backers. Many sales turned out to be total rip-offs. They were not only not traded at all, but some projects vanished with the money, never to be seen or heard from again.

So how do you know if you should invest in a particular token sale?

The amount of money that the project wishes to raise is an important consideration. A project that raises too little money will most likely be unable to develop a working product, whereas a project that raises too much money will likely not have enough investors to purchase the tokens on the market. The most crucial aspect is risk management. Never put all of your eggs in one basket, and avoid putting too much of your portfolio into a single IEO or ICO. They are classified as high risk.

Commissions

Performing multiple trades requires the payment of a higher commission. It is always better and less expensive for a market maker to place a new order in the order book rather than buy from the order book at a trading platform.

Don't create pressure

Start trading only when you have the best conditions to make the best decisions, and always know when and how to stop trading if necessary. Trading begins with a well-thought-out strategy! If you are under a lot of pressure, it will affect your decision-making ability. As a result, never rush.

Set targets and sale-orders

Set your goals by placing sell orders. You never know when a whale will pump up a coin in order to buy up the stock in the order book (and pay a lower price on the sale-order creator' side).

Buy the rumor, sell the news

When major news broadcasts publish news, this is usually the right time to sell the coin and not buying it!

Don't forget Murphy's Law

You made a profitable trade, but as is customary, the price skyrockets right after you sell. Don't give in to the temptation to change jobs. In other words, don't succumb to **FOMO** (Fear of Missing Out). You'll be fine as long as there are profits.

Don't let your ego rule your investments

The goal is to obtain PROFIT. Don't squander resources (time and money) attempting to demonstrate that you should have taken this or that position. Keep in mind that no trader only enters winning positions. The general rule is that the number of winning trades must exceed the number of lost trades.

Buy when the prices are low

Bear markets are sometimes the best times to make a profit, if coin is going down, that could mean it's the best time to buy in and make a profit over time. But make sure your plan is solid for the near future and you have some idea as to why the price drop is only temporary.

Buyers versus sellers

Consider the following hypothetical company. People who believe in the company purchase as many shares as they can at the $10 price.

However, in order to do so, there must also be people willing to sell their shares at this price. As a result, these people are skeptical that the price will rise. They would not sell if they thought it would! If a shareholder wishes to sell his shares, he is free to set his own price.

Assume someone lists his shares for sale at $12 each, and others want to buy at $10. In that case, both parties can agree on a price of $11 and meet in the middle. After the first trading day, the price of our donut shop is $11 per share. In many ways, this reflects how the market perceives our company.

This principle applies to cryptocurrencies in a similar way.

If you are a wise investor, you understand that you cannot learn everything simply by looking at the current price. Using historical data, you can estimate market sentiment. Is the current price too high or too low? What was the cost at the start of the day last year? Was there a price drop last quarter?

Bitcoin versus Ethereum

What is the difference and which cryptocurrency has the most promising future?

Earlier we explained how Bitcoin has tremendous long-term potential but how does it hold up against the number 2. Should you invest in both coins?

Bitcoin and Ethereum are the two largest crypto-currencies in market capitalization. Co-investors often choose to hold only one of the two in their portfolio. Despite that approach, these crypto currencies are still very different. What are the biggest differences? Why do people believe in one, and not the other? A few industry experts shed their light on the matter.

The bull-run of Ethereum in the past year

2021 has so far proved to be the year of Ethereum. The second crypto currency is rapidly approaching Bitcoin's market capitalization. For example, with a market capitalization of $501 billion, the currency is more valuable than U.S. investment bank JP Morgan at the time of writing.

Still, Bitcoin's biggest challenger has a long way to go if it wants to outgrow the market capitalization of Bitcoin (currently at $1 trillion). Recently, 1 Bitcoin was worth a whopping 13.25 Ethereum.

What exactly is Ethereum?

The Ethereum coin (ETH) is one of the coins with the most market capitalization. A high market capacity usually indicates that there is a lot of faith in a particular coin, and the Ethereum coin, like Bitcoin, has a lot of faith.

Whereas investors are skeptical about the future of Bitcoin, the future of the Ethereum coin appears to be bright for the time being. Indeed, the price of the Ethereum currency increased by more than 3000 percent in 2017.

Of course, the question is always whether investing in this virtual currency is still worthwhile. To be able to answer this question for yourself, this page will explain the principle of the currency. This way you can get an idea of what kind of currency it is and how you see the future of Ethereum.

How does it differ from Bitcoin?

Where Ripple, for example, focuses on making transactions faster for the financial market, the Ethereum coin focuses on the use of applications. The principle of Ethereum technology is to create a situation in which applications can be used without the intervention of a central authority. The applications that use this technology are also called DApps (or Decentralized Apps). The main advantage of applications using Ethereum technology is that there is basically no more data loss, manipulation of data, censorship within the application or downtime of the application.

The Ethereum currency's price is determined by more than just supply and demand among investors. The price is much more dependent on how much use is made of the DApps. A large number of businesses around the world support the Ethereum concept. As a result, it is not surprising that the currency's value has risen dramatically in 2017.

In the cryptocurrency market, Ethereum is still a relatively new coin. Ethereum's price has steadily increased since its inception in 2015. In 2017, the price of Ethereum increased by more than 3000 percent. This rise was easily explained as more international companies expressed interest in Ethereum.

Multinational corporations such as ING, Microsoft, BP, and Deloitte, to name a few, have already joined the Enterprise Ethereum Alliance (a partnership founded by Ethereum). The world's largest corporations are increasingly interested in collaborating with Ethereum. When more large companies that use the Ethereum network, the more trust there is in the currency. Higher confidence, of course, results in a higher exchange rate.

Purchasing Ethereum coins is similar to purchasing Bitcoin. Ethereum is linked to all of the well-known "Cryptocurrency exchanges," making it extremely simple to purchase the coin with other cryptocurrencies.

Purchasing Ethereum is similar to purchasing Bitcoin. Ethereum is linked to all of the well-known "Cryptocurrency exchanges," making it extremely simple to purchase the coin with other cryptocurrencies.

Ethereum coins can also be purchased with dollars through a number of international providers. Because not all exchanges charge a reasonable transaction fee, it is best to stick with the more well-known parties. The trick to buying Ethereum coins is, of course, to wait for the right time to buy. Many investors buy the coins when they are on the verge of falling in value.

The Ethereum cryptocurrency is relatively stable (as far as a Crypto currency can be stable). Despite the fact that the coin is relatively stable, investing in cryptocurrency is always risky.

As a result, only invest in Ethereum with funds that you can afford to lose. Many people believe that it is necessary to purchase full Ethereum coins; however, this is not the case. You can also purchase a half-coin or less.

Ethereum coins can be deposited using either an online or offline wallet. For the online deposit of Ethereum coins, you have a large number of online wallet providers to choose from.

Ethereum can be purchased online through exchanges such as Binance. Because Ethereum coins have a relatively high value, more people are opting to keep their coins safe and secure offline. You can also choose between a hardware wallet and a mobile wallet.

NFT and Ethereum

One of the reasons that Ethereum might see a good price increase in the next few years is because of NFT (non-fungible tokens).

NFTs have become wildly popular in a short time, including among artists hoping to earn a little pocket change in coronation times. Or pocket change? Some NFT art changes hands for millions.

The hype around non-fungible tokens is attracting newcomers to the crypto world. They are curious about what NFTs are or hope to become rich quickly by trading in digital art.

NFT sales run primarily over the Ethereum platform, like Bitcoin a decentralized network based on the blockchain concept. But just having a digital wallet full of ether - one of the most popular crypto currencies - doesn't get you there.

If you want to read more about NFT art and trading NFTs you can check out our book on the subject.

Summary:

- Ethereum is a decentralized platform that uses the blockchain technology pioneered by the mysterious Satoshi Nakamoto - a pseudonym - creator of Bitcoin.
- 'Whereas Bitcoin has discovered a way to transfer value digitally, directly from person to person, Ethereum is taking a different approach,' writes the niche website BTC.direct. The Ethereum network is said to be the foundation of a new type of Internet. Importantly, the Ethereum 'ecosystem' serves as a foundation for the development of decentralized applications (DAPPs) and smart contracts.
- DAPPs would be much more privacy-friendly and secure than current centralized Internet applications. They are also uncensorable.

How do big Ethereum investors see the future?

Tally Greenberg, head of business development at software company Allnodes has the following to say about Ethereum:

'The technological advantage and utility of the Ethereum ecosystem is far greater than that of Bitcoin, and I think investors are beginning to see that too. There is currently more than $75 billion invested in DeFi projects on the Ethereum blockchain - just a month ago

it was $40 billion. Just the smart contracts supported by the network offer endless possibilities and should be enough for Ethereum to have a competitive advantage over Bitcoin.'

Steve Ehrlich, CEO and founder of cryptocurrency brokerage Voyager Digital:

"I believe Ethereum offers better prospects due to its utility, functionality, and ecosystem." Clients of Voyager (crypto asset broker, ed.) who own both Bitcoin and Ether have begun to hold more Ether in recent months. We are also seeing that our larger investors are becoming more comfortable with Ether's risk/reward profile. The Ethereum blockchain is powering the most developed ecosystem for decentralized finance and NFTs, which are all gaining popularity. Ethereum will also receive a -interesting- upgrade in the near future."

"There is anticipation that ETH will be recognized by institutional investors," **says Megan Kaspar, managing director of crypto investment firm Magnetic.**

"Ether, I believe, will gain traction. When investors become aware of the technological opportunities, capital flows will shift to Ether. In the long run, technical and fundamental analyses show that Ether has a higher upside potential than Bitcoin."

What is the difference between Bitcoin and Ethereum?

The Ethereum network allows developers to build their own decentralized applications; Bitcoin does not have this.

Another difference is that the creator of Ethereum is known, while that of Bitcoin is not.

Supply determines the price of Bitcoin (unlike fiat currency, the supply Bitcoins is scarce and finite). With Ether, however, there are other factors at play: for example, the network allows start-ups to issue a token for their own blockchain project.

Right now, investors should have both Bitcoin and Ethereum in their portfolios.

Bitcoin has a strong chance of remaining the world's leading crypto asset, while Ethereum has a sTrong chance of becoming the world's leading distributed software development platform.

As a result, if you want to get the most out of your portfolio, **invest in both now.**

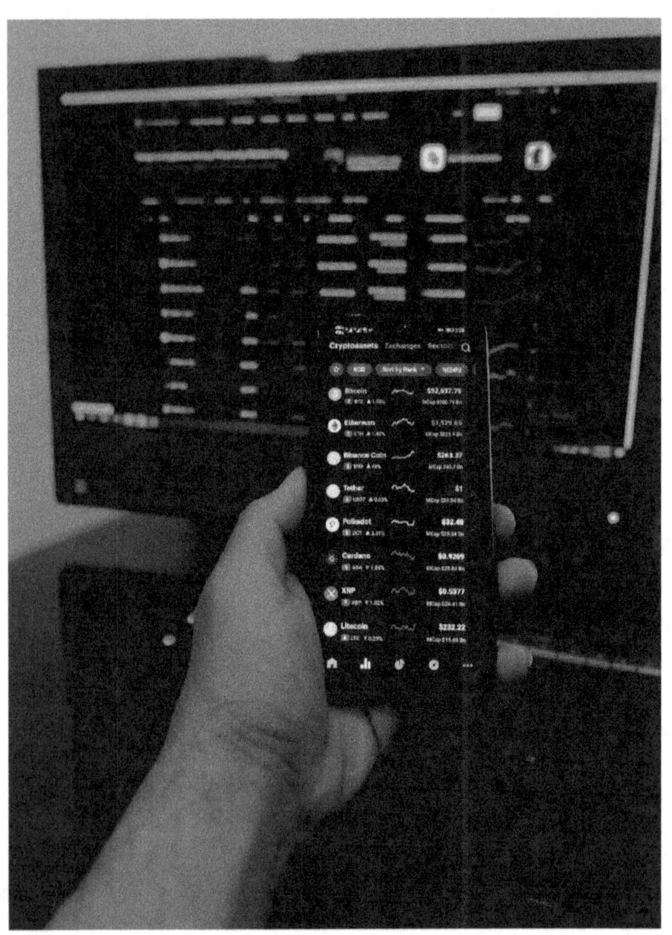

Why does Ripple get attention?

Aside from Bitcoin, there are a plethora of other cryptocurrencies that may be far more lucrative in terms of returns than the well-known Bitcoin. Ripple (XRP), is one of the cryptocurrencies with a massive market cap. Since the end of 2017, the price of the Ripple currency has risen dramatically, and it continues to fluctuate significantly to this day.

You may be wondering, "Is the Ripple a good coin to invest in?" In order to provide a satisfactory answer, we will delve deeper into everything Ripple in this chapter.

What is Ripple?

Let us begin by answering the question, "What is Ripple?" Cryptocurrencies were developed in the aftermath of the economic crisis, partly to reduce the influence of banks on economic transactions. Whereas most cryptocurrencies today still base their profiles on this concept, the Ripple coin does not. Ripple, on the other hand, is a centralized currency designed to allow financial institutions (including banks) and international transactions to be completed more quickly.

Ripple is already working on a payment system solution for much of Santander's, Reise Bank's, BBVA's, Bank of America's, and UniCredit's banking traffic, among others. They already have a 40% stake in the payment system for banks in Asia.

Ripple's technology is expected to pique the interest of an increasing number of banks. As a result, the number of banks that will use this technology is expected to grow rapidly.

Of course, "speeding up international transactions" does not sound very clear right now. The principle of the Ripple technology will be explained in greater detail using a brief example: There is a currency difference when a customer wants to make a transaction from a Spanish bank (e.g., Santander) to an American bank (e.g. Bank of America).

The Spanish customer transfers the amount in euros, and this arrives in dollars at the American bank. In order to carry out these transactions, Santander Bank has an account with Bank of America and Bank of America has an account with Santander bank, so-called nostro and vostro accounts.

Making a Spanish payment to a U.S. bank takes a long time due to the many links in this process. Ripple focuses on speeding up this process, by completing transactions in Ripple currency.

Making a payment now no longer takes several days, but only a few seconds. Not only does this reduce transaction costs for banks, but customers of the banks can also complete their transactions faster.

The Ripple lawsuit

The SEC filed a surprise lawsuit against Ripple and two of its executives, co-founder Chris Larsen and CEO Brad Garlinghouse, in December. The regulator claims that continuing to sell XRP to individual investors violates securities laws.

The SEC hopes to strengthen its case by demonstrating that Ripple purposefully manipulated the cryptocurrency's XRP price expectation with strategically timed announcements.

So far, Larsen and Garlinghouse's analysis of crypto wallets has revealed that massive amounts of XRP were delivered to exchanges based on foreign soil. However, Ripple "did not hand over any non-U.S. based digital asset account documents or otherwise explain the significance of these XRP transfers," according to the SEC letter.

"Although the SEC has also attempted to obtain this information directly from Ripple, Ripple recently informed the SEC that Ripple does not have it either, leaving the only avenue for investigation offshore," the letter explains.

However, it appears that the investigations are not off to a good start, with requests to nine different foreign regulators returning empty-handed. According to the letter, two regulators refused to help, and three others refused to allow the SEC to publish their communications. Only one regulator suggested that the

SEC could use conversations between the two parties to strengthen its case.

If the court grants Ripple's motion, the SEC would be required to make cease and desist requests to foreign regulators, effectively ending this line of inquiry.

11:20
Bitcoin
$36,588.28
-0.02%
$38,769.84

What is the price of Ripple?

Now that we've covered the fundamentals and the recent news surrounding the lawsuit against Ripple, let's get to the bottom of the question: What is the price of Ripple? Ripple was founded in 2012 with the goal of speeding up financial transactions. Whereas the price was initially stable (low), it has risen significantly since the end of 2017.

Ripple became a billion-dollar company almost immediately as a result of the price increase. The owners of Ripple still manage a large portion of the market capacity, so the public has only a limited amount of market capacity.

The price rise can be explained by the fact that Ripple has contracted with a number of large customers in the financial world. These include customers such as Bank of America and Royal Bank of Scotland. In addition, Ripple has the support of many multinational companies, including Google. In January 2018, the price first stood at $3.10 per Ripple.

The price increase can be explained by the fact that Ripple has signed contracts with a number of large financial customers. Customers include Bank of America and the Royal Bank of Scotland. Furthermore, Ripple has the backing of many multinational corporations, including Google. In January 2018, the price was $3.10 per Ripple.

How to buy Ripple

Are you already a little excited? Then you must be asking yourself, where can I buy Ripple? In the beginning, it was difficult to buy Ripple with dollars or euros. Fortunately, more and more options for this have emerged recently.

When buying Ripple coins with dollars, there are often high transaction fees. It is therefore advisable to first convert the dollars to a more common digital currency (for example, Bitcoin (BTC) or Ethereum (ETH) and then purchase the Ripple coins through an exchange like Binance.

Cardano: the smart coin

Cardano has made a name for itself in the world of virtual currencies in a relatively short period of time. Cardano has already entered the top five cryptocurrency coins in early 2018. As a result, the coin is already more valuable than well-known coins like NEM and Litecoin.

Although it is impossible to predict a coin's future, cryptocurrency experts have high hopes for the Cardano coin. As a result, it is expected that this coin will overtake the number two spot in the near future. Of course, the question now is how to explain the Cardano coin's success.

The success of Cardano, according to its developers, can be attributed to the fact that it is the only virtual currency based on academic mathematical theories.

A collaboration of several international universities resulted in the creation of the Cardano coin. The Cardano coin's creators include renowned academics from universities such as Athens, Edinburgh, and Connecticut, among others. The Cardano cryptocurrency is based on a number of (highly regarded) academic mathematics theories. As such, the coin is named after mathematician Gerolamo Cardano, one of history's most famous and influential mathematicians.

Of course, a virtual currency based on mathematical theories sounds extremely intriguing, but what does this mean in practice for the currency's quality? Cardano's CEO is also the former CEO and developer of the Ethereum cryptocurrency.

He noticed that most new cryptocurrencies launch new coins quickly and, as a result, do not spend enough time developing the entire concept.

According to him, as a result of this, many virtual coins end up making promises that they cannot keep in practice.

According to Charles Hoskinson, this ultimately leads to less trust in the cryptocurrency market as a whole. The Cardano coin was created to restore this trust.

Cardano employs a team of academics to ensure that the promises made for the coin are kept in practice. Responsibilities within the project are delegated to academics who are experts in that specific field.

Of course, having a good team is critical for a virtual currency, but it is ultimately about the technology behind the coin. The primary distinction between current cryptocurrencies and Cardano is that the Cardano coin operates on the 'formal verification' principle.

Smart contracts based on 'informal verification' are increasingly being used with virtual currencies today, often resulting in contracts that are untested or do not fully function.

Mathematical theories are used to test the 'formal verification' of the Cardano coin. To ensure the security of the coin, the team uses the programming language 'Haskell'. Experts consider Haskell to be the most secure programming language.

Cardano has also created its own 'Ouroboros' technique, which is based on the well-known 'Proof of Stake (POS)' method. The 'Proof of Stake' principle dictates that the coin, like Bitcoin, cannot be mined. The Proof of Stake principle states that keeping coins in a wallet increases the number of coins (also called "staking").

Cardano is not the only virtual currency that employs the 'Proof of Stake' method; leading coins such as NEO, Dash, and Stratis do as well. While the technique is obviously extremely intriguing, it also poses some security risks. Cardano's Ouroboros technique ensures that these security risks are eliminated.

What is the price of Cardano?

It has been possible to purchase Cardano ICO since 2015, this period only stopped in January 2017. For a long time, Cardano showed a stable price around $0.02.

From the beginning of November 2017, the Cardano price showed several fluctuations, a steady rise was evident.

In early 2018, the virtual currency reached a phenomenal rise, the value was then at over $1.21 each for a short period of time.

Although the Cardano coin is still considered a relatively young coin on the cryptocurrency market, more and more leading traders are expressing confidence in the future of Cardano. Clearly visible, therefore, is an increase in Cardano's market capacity.

How to buy Cardano?
In the meantime, are you also convinced of a successful future for Cardano? Then you can choose to also purchase a number of these coins.

In the beginning of 2021, the price of these coins will fluctuate between $0.80 and $2.40 each, so you can already get invested for a small amount of money. Buying Cardano coins can be done on the exchange of Binance.

To be able to purchase Cardano, you can first buy Bitcoins and then convert them into Cardano. However, nowadays it is also possible to buy Cardano directly.

Purchasing these Bitcoins can be done for example through a platform like Coinbase.

Nano

Although the coin's name may allude to something insignificant, Nano cryptocurrency (NANO, formerly known as RaiBlocks) has high ambitions to surpass the goal of Bitcoin. As a means of daily payment, Nano aspires to be an alternative to both fiat currencies and the dominant crypto currencies. Such systems are frequently stagnated by various technological constraints, but the organization of Nano presents its "cure" in the blockchain architecture, which provides secure and instantaneous transactions without cost.

What exactly is Nano?
The Nano team focuses on Bitcoin in its white paper as the first cryptocurrency to gain widespread acceptance and introduce the public to the blockchain. Bitcoin, according to these developers, commits several major sins that no cryptocurrency should commit.

- **Scalability is limited.** The scalability issue stems from the limited capacity of blockchain blocks to store data. It effectively reduces the number of transactions per second that the blockchain can handle, especially as the technology matures and the number of users on the platform grows. It has also effectively turned a spot in a block into a "commodity," with the average Bitcoin transaction cost considered unacceptable by many users.

- **Long latency.** Existing computational latency with Bitcoin and other cryptocurrencies is described as excessive and one of the causes of long confirmation times. Nano is attempting to improve in this area as well.

- **Power consumption is inefficient.** For example, because Bitcoin's Proof of Work (PoW) consensus model requires an average of 260 kWh per transaction, the entire network would require approximately 27 TWh per year. As an alternative, Nano proposes abandoning distributed consensus protocols such as PoW and Proof of Stake (PoS) and instead providing each user with his or her own blockchain. It may reduce competition among owners of computational systems and allow the use of less demanding ones for the same purpose.

All of these features, when combined, should theoretically provide the Nano platform with unlimited scaling, as well as faster and smoother transactions and lower energy consumption as a bonus for users.

This still contributes to the fact that Bitcoin is an excellent store of value in the long-term due to its technical limitations. However as a payment system, Nano would be far more superior.

What is the price of Nano

Nano's market capitalization is $247,049,170 as of November 2018. By 2021, the market capitalization can exceed $1,441,775,355. The current value is a drop from the all-time high of over $4 billion in early 2018.

The total and circulating supply of Nano is 133,248,290 NANO, and no new tokens are being created. The taps-based system, which closed in October 2017, was used for the initial distribution of tokens. Nano can be purchased on cryptocurrency exchanges like Binance and HitBTC.

Stellar Lumens

Jed McCaleb founded both Stellar Lumens and Ripple, which are digital currencies. Although they are based on the same premise, they are not the same, as Lumens focuses on assisting individuals in transferring money rather than institutions. McCaleb has taken a more active approach to the common man with Lumens, as opposed to his predecessor's more corporate approach.

The Stellar network is the actual decentralized peer-to-peer framework, while Lumens (XLM) is the network's token. The network was founded in 2014, and as of May 2021, Stellar Lumens had risen to the 14th position among the most popular crypto-currencies. Stellar's all-time high price was $0.93 in January 2018, but it is now only $0.06.

What is the purpose of Stellar Lumens?

Lumens were created to assist people in overcoming the challenges of cross-border transactions. Long transaction times and high fees are two of these impediments. Lumens sought to alleviate these issues for residential users by providing a quick and inexpensive way to send money around the world.

Stellar Lumens' creators recognize that not everyone in our world has easy access to financial services, and even if they do, they may be prohibitively expensive. As a result, the team is committed to providing financial services to anyone anywhere in the world who has an active internet connection and some basic hardware resources.

Lumens are the tokens that the larger Stellar network uses to send money and convert currencies. The network is a peer-to-peer network that is decentralized.

Lumens enable one type of currency to be sent by one peer and received by another as another type of currency. It will pass through several currencies on its way to the recipient. The Stellar network accomplishes this by determining whether a direct currency pair exchange is available.

If not, it can check to see if a Lumens holder's initial currency is in demand, and once it has the Lumens, it can look for a number of Lumens plus the final currency. This enables a simple value transaction between currencies that do not have a common traded pair.

All of this is made possible by "anchors" in the Stellar network. Anchors facilitate currency exchange within the network by being able to hold a deposit as well as issue credit in another currency. This process is incredibly fast because all anchors are on the same network, the Stellar network.

Although Lumens have intrinsic value, the primary function of tokens is to serve as a bridge between different currencies. As such, it would be beneficial to consider it as more than just money. Its ability to convert currencies for users and do so quickly distinguishes it from standard fiat currencies that are commonly referred to as 'real money.'

IBM chose Stellar Lumens to assist in the development of World Wire, which allows financial institutions to send money around the world at a much lower and faster cost than ever before. Stellar Lumens gained credibility and exposure to the traditional financial world by collaborating with IBM.

Is Stellar Lumens worth the investment?

Stellar Lumens are not mineable. Stellar, on the other hand, controls the supply of Lumens. Initially, 100 billion Lumens were created, with the supply increasing by 1% per year for five years until the Stellar community voted against it.

Stellar took the community's advice and cut the number of existing Lumens in half, to 50 billion, vowing never to create more. Only about 20 billion of these 50 billion are still in circulation, with the rest held by the SDF for development and promotional purposes.

Stellar Lumens transactions between accounts are conducted using a consensus protocol because there is no mining.

With a large supply of Lumens, a relatively low coin price, and the fact that it is not regarded as a good store of value, it may currently be a risky investment when compared to other crypto assets such as Ethereum, Bitcoin, and Link.

However, if an increasing number of people around the world begin to use Lumens to transfer money, the story could change dramatically.

A Lumens transaction costs 0.00001 XLM, making it extremely cheap. When you buy Lumens through online exchanges, the site where you buy them will charge you a fee.

Coinbase, for example, charges between 0.99 and 2.99 euros for each purchase between 1 and 200 euros. When using a debit card, there is an additional 3.99 percent fee. Exchanges such as Kraken have much lower fees, typically around 0.26 percent, but these are still additional fees on top of the actual coins.

Binance Futures

The concept works as follows in futures trading, such as Binance Future. You place a wager on a price prediction. As a result, futures are a derivative (or a derivative) of a cryptocurrency. Futures trading is becoming increasingly popular for a variety of important reasons. The following are the reasons:

Futures trading allows you to make a lot of money even in a market where prices are dropping.

Working with levers (leverage) considerably increases profit opportunities (and with it also the risk!).

There are a few more benefits to mention, but these two are by far the most important.

When you own cryptocurrency, it increases in value when prices rise and decreases in value when prices fall. This is not a difficult task. However, in a bear market, it is impossible to profit from that cryptocurrency. At best, you can sell everything at a price ceiling, wait for a price drop, and then try to buy at a price floor.

However, futures trading allows you to profit even in a down market. You can, for example, place a bet on the prediction of a price drop. If the price falls in the future, you'll get paid for it.

On the other hand, of course, you'll lose money the moment the predicted price drop doesn't happen, and the prices rise.

Futures trading allows you to take advantage of the so-called leverage effect. This allows you to multiply the effects of your trades up to 125 times. This is also why futures trading in general is only appropriate for more experienced crypto traders.

When you use leverage, that factor is applied to every dollar profit or loss you make. This has a lot of potential, but it also has a lot of risk. As a result, it is critical to proceed with caution and forethought.

You can increase the impact of your trades by using leverage. Leverage on futures trades can be set between 1x and 125x. So, if you set a leverage of 20x (the standard setting for futures), you'll be able to open a position of no less than 200 USDT with 10 USDT.

This allows you to quickly trade with large sums of money, which is why it's critical that you understand how the liquidation process behind these positions works. The greater your position, the less leverage you have. Otherwise, it's also true that the smaller your position, the more leverage you have.

The risk of Binance Futures

If you have been involved in investments on a regular basis, you will be aware that investing entails a certain amount of risk. Shares, bonds, commodities, futures contracts, and cryptocurrencies all have a value at the time of purchase that can rise or fall. As a result, this is referred to as investment risk.

Investing in government bonds or index funds is generally less risky than investing in individual stocks. Stock trading is often less risky than cryptocurrency trading. As you are probably aware, the cryptocurrency market is extremely volatile.

When you begin trading futures and add a leverage factor, the risk is multiplied by the leverage factor. It's not for nothing that futures trading is best suited to more experienced traders. The opportunity is unprecedentedly large, but so is the risk.

The general rule is that the greater the risk, the greater the profit margin. And vice versa: the lower the profit margin, the lower the risk.

It may be clear that futures trading opens up a new territory in which opportunities and threats lie in wait. In any case it offers opportunities you would not have on the normal (spot) trading market, partly thanks to the leverage principle.

Nevertheless trading futures also entails a considerable risk, as a result of which it is not suitable for every trader. Whether or not futures trading is something for you is something that sTrongly depends on your risk profile, the experience you've gained in crypto trading and the knowledge you possess. And of course a luck factor will apply to your success with Binance Futures trading.

Solana

Solana is one of the cryptocurrency market's fastest rising stars. Since the beginning of 2021, the altcoin has increased by nearly 3,000 percent. While SOL was worth about $1.50 on January 1, it is now worth more than $40 at the time of writing. Why has Solana risen so dramatically?

Solana's growth is most likely due to the network's ability to handle a large number of transactions per second.

For example, Bitcoin (BTC) can only handle 7 transactions per second (TPS) without the assistance of layer-2 solutions, and Ethereum (ETH) can only handle 15 to 18 TPS at the moment.

As the market expands, these networks become increasingly congested, resulting in higher transaction costs.

SOL is the Solana blockchain's crypto currency. It is used for the following purposes:

Solana strike: Solana allows for inflationary rewards for users who strike SOL in exchange for network support. Solana is a delegated Proof-of-Stake consensus network. In other words, SOL holders can delegate a portion of their SOL assets to a validator, who is in charge of processing transactions and running the network.

Transaction fees: SOL crypto currency can be used to perform smart contracts and transactions.

Governance: The SOL token will be used to vote on specific proposals within the Solana community and organization.

The total number of SOL distributed is now over 16,500,000 SOL (3.35 percent). At this time, the total amount is 488,634,933 SOL, of which 11,365,067 SOL have been burned (burned) out of the initial maximum amount of 500,000,000 SOL.

Indeed, SOL has a deflationary monetary policy in which the SOL quantity is reduced (burning) to make the long-term strike more appealing. Scarcity worsens over time.

Why should you invest in Solana?

Solana has already formed innovative technology partnerships with FTX, Arweave, Pocket Network, Fortmatic, dFuse, LoanSnap, Akash, Chainlink, Hummingbot, and Civic, among others. These technological collaborations will strengthen Solona's network effect.

Multicoin Capital, Foundation Capital, Distributed Global, CMCC, Blocktower Capital, NGC Capital, and Rockaway Ventures are among the major venture capital firms that have invested in Solana (SOL).

If you want to actively use the network to develop decentralized applications based on Solana, you will need to have SOL. If you want to earn SOL for free and invest in the future of Solana, you can stake SOL. To do so, however, you will need to invest money in SOL first.

Invest only with venture capital in SOL that you can afford to lose. It is a new project and it can certainly fail. Always start with a good understanding of Bitcoin's value proposition before investing in other projects.

EOS

EOS has been in the news a lot recently, as it is frequently compared to the well-known Ethereum. Although a comparison may not be the best word to use. EOS is already being regarded as the new Ethereum. But why is this the case, and who is behind this initiative?

Scalability is a term used frequently in the cryptocurrency world. Bitcoin and Ethereum are by far the most popular coins, which creates complications. Transactions are becoming increasingly difficult to complete due to the large number of users. Ethereum remains faster than Bitcoin, but it is still very slow. This is especially true when you consider that Visa, for example, can process thousands of transactions per second.

EOS currently relies on the Ethereum network, but it intends to create its own. By making a few changes, this coin's scalability should improve. Usability is a key word in EOS. Whereas Ethereum requires lessons to learn the programming language, this crypto currency does not.

Dan Larimer

Dan Larimer is the project's big name, and he's developed a number of technologies over the years.

Dan is the creator of the well-known projects Bitshares and Steem. At the time, Bitshares was a revolutionary exchange. Apart from the fact that this exchange was decentralized, there was something else going on. Dan pioneered horizontal scalability, which enabled millions of transactions per second. This is precisely what EOS required, among other things, in order to defeat its archrival Ethereum. Bithares was later disbanded, and Dan devoted himself to a new endeavor.

He was also the brains behind Steem. Steem was revolutionary in that it introduced a blockchain-based social media platform.

Furthermore, the Steem community could earn money in the form of Steem Dollars. He reduced transaction costs by implementing this. After all, users can interact with one another for free. He abandoned Steem in order to concentrate on EOS.

Dan wishes to incorporate the knowledge he gained from these projects into this crypto currency. This coin should make it simple for users to create decentralized apps on the EOS network. By increasing scalability, no other measures, such as Bitcoin's so-called hard forks, are required. When using this network, there is also no need to pay transaction fees.

It should be a network for everyone, without having to have technical knowledge. In addition to scalability and eliminating transaction costs, Dan wants to adopt another technology. The delegated proof of stake (DPOS), which he himself introduced.

With this system, certain people are designated by voting. The more EOS tokens someone owns, the more voting power. The people who are designated can make decisions regarding the network. If a person does a wrong job, they can be ousted from their position.

It all depends on whether this project is going to succeed if it is going to rise significantly. Founder Dan is a frontrunner in this project and we have to take him at his word. In addition, it is important that it does not take too long.

EOS must be the first with a reliable and fast network, better than the Ethereum network.

TRON

TRON has been active since 2017-08-28. In this relatively short time, an enormous amount of developments have already happened. The price is determined by supply and demand. However, there is a maximum supply available.

For this coin that is and there is currently only a circulating supply of 71,660,220,128. If we look at the total cryptocurrency market, it is at 23 in the total market. The all time high stands at $0.23, since this huge milestone, it has dropped 49.42%.

Tron is the cryptocurrency designed to advance the entertainment, gaming and media industry. It was founded by Justin Sun in the year 2017 and is very suitable for:

- More easily selling content that is still in development

- Peer to peer technology

- Reducing fees to intermediaries

- Building decentralized applications

- Storing data

- Using it as a means of payment for entertainment services

So Tron is a blockchain that uses three different layers. These layers are the **storage**, **core** and **application** layers. Tron uses the Google protobuf protocol which allows it to work indirectly with different programming languages. The team of Tron consists of consultants, investors and experienced developers. The goal of Tron is to have all kinds of services using Tron so that everyone can buy from it because they all have it.

TRX expectation in the short term is very difficult to predict. It can be concluded that the price of this currency is linked to the news and developments. How many times has it happened that Elon Musk posted a Tweet and the entire cryptocurrency market showed a movement.

This is a development that is actually unpredictable. but there is certainly great potential for the practical application of this crypto coin, and to ensure that you invest at the right time, it is wise to keep an eye on the news surrounding crypto currencies.

Large companies becoming interested in the application of crypto in their business successes are often a good indication of a rise in value.

Chainlink

Chainlink (LINK) as a company has the primary goal of helping companies apply blockchain properly. That may sound very general, but they have a specific solution for this. Chainlink builds oracles that allow you to load information and data into blockchains and smart contracts. For example, you can link a live feed of data from the weather in the Netherlands to other data via a blockchain. They are not that far yet, the oracles are now mainly used by companies that offer decentralized, financial services.

In concrete terms, Chainlink is a company that manifests itself as a total solution provider in the field of blockchain implementation within large companies or data processors. They are now increasingly being called upon for DeFi applications and the company's potential therefore seems enormous.

The associated token is intended to reward users who keep nodes running and power the network. There are rumors that Chainlink is developing a method to produce these coins. This means that you lock in your coins and earn interest on them for a set period of time.

Chainlink's oracle ensures that data from various sources (other blockchains, back-end systems, payment systems, market data, and so on) is processed in such a way that it can be used in a standalone blockchain.

Chainlink is a smart contract-focused platform. These are blockchain-based contracts that are programmed and concluded. This frequently occurs between two parties, where the smart contract examines the data and conditions to which both parties are bound.

If both parties have met their contractual obligations, the smart contract will automatically approve and execute the contract. If the contract is not approved, everyone's money will be returned.

The emergence and utility of this smart contract is what makes Chainlink so intriguing.

Having a smart contract executed is of course very interesting, especially because these are automatically programmed on the blockchain based on rules that are digitally added to the smart contract. Because everything is transparent in this case, you don't need the other party's trust. As a result, trust is programmed into the blockchain.

However, there are drawbacks to this smart contract, because it frequently requires data, which must be retrieved from companies or through databases. And before such a smart contract can approve "agreements and conditions," the data must be present.

This is precisely where Chainlink aspires to be the solution. Chainlink has recently developed an Oracle that allows businesses and institutions to connect to Chainlink's Oracle using an API KEY, allowing data to be retrieved.

Previously, retrieving this type of data was only possible if the organization from which the data came only took action.

As a result, the blockchain was never truly decentralized. As a result of the connection between the decentralized Chainlink Oracle and the counterparty, each smart contract can be controlled without the involvement of a third party.

Obviously, the marketing team didn't spend a lot of time agonizing over the token's name, but it did turn out to be a catchy name, shall we say.

At the same time, LINK does not require marketing to gain attention. A 730 percent return in the first three quarters of 2019 drew a lot of attention in the crypto industry.

When you're as successful as LINK, the world is talking about you regardless of how much time and effort you put into marketing your own cryptocurrency.

Chainlink is the classic example of an ICO that turned out incredibly nicely. For both the company Chainlink and the LINK token, and of course for all the investors who put the initial millions on the table together. Had you participated for 100 euros in 2017? Then today you would have grabbed just $3,700 on that. Not bad, right? Chainlink's share price went from 0.09 cents to over $5.

And even though past results are no guarantee for the future, the potential for Chainlink (and with it also LINK) is limitless. As more and more companies invest in blockchain and look for solutions to integrate their datasets with other companies' datasets, Chainlink's oracle solution will prove to be an incredibly inventive one.

And as Chainlink's technology becomes more popular, more node operators are needed. The more node operators that are needed, the more they get paid together. And the more they get paid together, the more demand there will be for LINK.

Conclusion

You should have a good idea of how to conduct your own risk assessment when it comes to investing in cryptocurrencies by now. And, before you begin, make sure you have a plan, do your research, and are eager to learn the value of the coin you wish to invest in.

One of the most important rules of investing is to educate yourself on the hype before you begin. Instead of paying for someone else's profit with the next pump and dump scheme, make sure your investment is calculated.

And, if you want to make huge profits with day trading, making real money from the previously mentioned pump and dump schemes, make sure you get a reliable source of information. There are numerous free and paid investment groups that can provide you with solid insights on coins with high short-term trading potential.

If you like the sound of a high risk, high reward approach to cryptocurrencies, Binance Futures trading could be an option.

Let us know what you think of the book, and if it has proven to be useful, please leave us a review so that others can benefit as well.

Thank you for reading our book, and good luck with your future investments!

Our books

Check out our other book to learn more about NFTs, NFT trading and selling, how to make profit and essential tips and strategies for a fail-proof start in the NFT universe.

Join the exclusive Stellar Moon Publishing Circle!

You'll get instant access to the mailing list with updates from our experts every week!

Sign up here today:

https://campsite.bio/stellarmoonpublishing

93

www.ingramcontent.com/pod-product-compliance
Lightning Source LLC
Chambersburg PA
CBHW051445150726
48000CB00005B/2254